Poetry Reprint Series

MOUNT ZION

or

In Touch with the Infinite

by John Betjeman

St. James Press
London

St. Martin's Press
New York

Copyright 1916 by The Poetry Bookshop
Reprinted 1975 by St. James Press
All rights reserved. For information, write:
St. James Press Ltd., la Montagu Mews North, London W1H 1AJ
or
St. Martin's Press, Inc., 175 Fifth Ave., New York, N.Y. 10010
Printed in the U.S.A.
ISBN 0 900997 21 5
Library of Congress Catalog Card Number: 75-10005
This reprint first published in the U.K. and U.S.A. in 1975

MOUNT ZION was first published in 1931. The cover was of light pink cloth; lettering and borders were in brown printed on light blue paper; the illustrations were in blue, pink, and brown. This reprint is photographed from the copy in the British Library, London.

Poetry Reprint Series: Set One

MOUNT ZION

OR

IN TOUCH WITH THE INFINITE

MOUNT ZION

MOUNT ZION

OR

IN TOUCH WITH THE INFINITE

BY

JOHN BETJEMAN

LONDON
THE JAMES PRESS

Printed in England
and published by The James Press
at 3 Culross Street, W.1

SEZINCOTE   MORETON-IN-MARSH

CONSTANTLY
UNDER THOSE MINARETS
I have been raised from the deepest depression
and spent the happiest days
of my life.

MRS. ARTHUR DUGDALE

therefore, the hostess of Sezincote, I run risk
of alienating
by dedicating to her this precious,
hyper-sophisticated book.

THE AUTHOR

is indebted to the Editors of *The London Mercury,
The Captain, The Week-End Review, The Cherwell,
The Architectural Review* and *The Calvinistic
Argus* for permission to reprint some of these
poems. He is also indebted to Mr. C. D. Fry of
Batsfords for the loan of the illustration on page
25 and to Lord Dufferin for the loan of the book
containing the illustration on the cover. To de
Cronin Hastings is due the greatest debt, for
his illustrations express the beauty of suburbia
far more than the verse; they appear on pages
21, 35, 40, 44, 46 and 55. Mr. Edward James
and the printers must be deeply thanked for
their forbearance and understanding. The author
is also grateful for his very good friends.

Contents

DEATH IN LEAMINGTON

SHE DIED in the upstairs bedroom
  By the light of the ev'ning star
That shone through the plate glass window
  From over Leamington Spa.

Beside her the lonely crochet
  Lay patiently and unstirred,
But the fingers that would have work'd it
  Were dead as the spoken word.

And Nurse came in with the tea-things
  Breast high 'mid the stands and chairs—
But Nurse was alone with her own little soul,
  And the things were alone with theirs.

She bolted the big round window,
  She let the blinds unroll,
She set a match to the mantel,
  She covered the fire with coal,

And "Tea!" she said in a tiny voice.
"Wake up! It's nearly *five*."
Oh! Chintzy, Chintzy cheeriness,
Half dead and half alive!

Do you know that the stucco is peeling?
Do you know that the heart will stop?
From those yellow Italianate arches
Do you hear the plaster drop?

Nurse looked at the silent bedstead,
At the gray, decaying face,
As the calm of a Leamington ev'ning
Drifted into the place.

She moved the table of bottles
Away from the bed to the wall;
And tiptoeing gently over the stairs
Turned down the gas in the hall.

HYMN

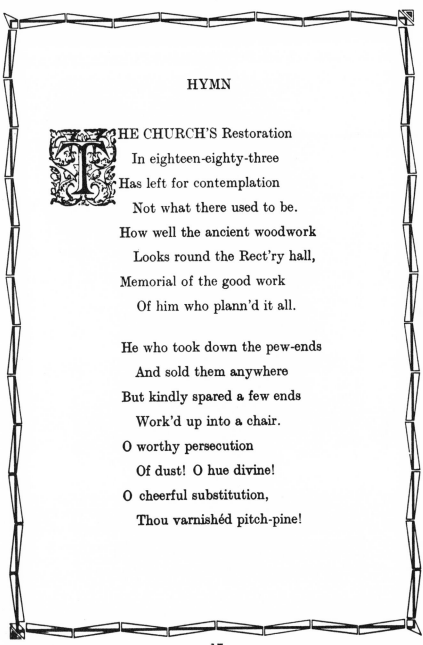

THE CHURCH'S Restoration
    In eighteen-eighty-three
Has left for contemplation
    Not what there used to be.
How well the ancient woodwork
    Looks round the Rect'ry hall,
Memorial of the good work
    Of him who plann'd it all.

He who took down the pew-ends
    And sold them anywhere
But kindly spared a few ends
    Work'd up into a chair.
O worthy persecution
    Of dust! O hue divine!
O cheerful substitution,
    Thou varnishéd pitch-pine!

17

Church furnishing! Church furnishing!
  Come, MOWBRAY, swell the praise!
He gave the brass for burnishing,
  He gave the thick red baize,
He gave the new addition,
  Pull'd down the dull old aisle,
—To pave the sweet transition
  He gave th' encaustic tile.

Of marble brown and veinéd
  He did the pulpit make;
He order'd windows stainéd
  Light red and crimson lake.
Sing on, with hymns uproarious,
  Ye humble and aloof,
Look up! and oh how glorious
  He has restored the roof!

THE 'VARSITY STUDENTS' RAG

'M AFRAID the fellows in Putney rather wish they had
The social ease and manners of a 'varsity undergrad,
For tho' they're awf'lly decent and up to a lark as a rule
You want to have the 'varsity touch after a public school.

> *Chorus:* We had a rag at Monico's,
> We had a rag at the Troc.,
> And the one we had at the Berkeley
> Gave the customers quite a shock.
> *Then* we went to the Popular,
> And after that—oh my!
> I *wish* you'd seen the rag we had
> In the Grill Room at the Cri.

I started a rag in Putney at our Frothblower's Branch down there;

We got in a damn'd ol' lorry and drove to Trafalgar
Square;
And we each had a couple of toy balloons and made the
hell of a din,
And I saw a bobby at Parson's Green who looked like
running us in.

Chorus: We, etc.

But that's nothing to the rag we had at the college the
other night;
We'd gallons and gallons of cider—and I got frightfully
tight.
And then we smash'd up ev'rything, and what was the
funniest part
We smashed some rotten old pictures which were price-
less works of art.

Chorus: We, etc.

There's something about a 'varsity man that distinguishes
 him from a cad:
You can tell by his tie and blazer he's a 'varsity undergrad,
And you know that he's always ready and up to a bit of
 a lark,
With a toy balloon and a whistle and some cider after
 dark.

Chorus: We, etc.

THE CITY

BUSINESS MEN with awkward hips,
And dirty jokes upon their lips,
And large behinds and jingling chains,
And riddled teeth and riddling brains,
And plump white fingers made to curl
Round some anæmic city girl,
And so lend colour to the lives
And old suspicions of their wives.

Young men who wear on office stools
The ties of minor public schools,
Each learning how to be a sinner
And tell 'a good one' after dinner,
And so discover it is rather
Fun to go one more than father.
But father, son and clerk join up
To talk about the Football Cup.

AN EIGHTEENTH-CENTURY CALVINISTIC HYMN

THANK GOD my Afflictions are such
That I cannot lie down on my Bed,
And if I but take to my Couch
    I incessantly Vomit and Bleed.

I am not too sure of my Worth,
    Indeed it is tall as a Palm;
But what Fruits can it ever bring forth
    When Leprosy sits at the Helm?

Though Torment's the Soul's Goal's Rewards
    The contrary's Proof of my Guilt,
While Dancing, Backgammon and Cards
    Are among the worst Symptoms I've felt.

Oh! I bless the good LORD for my Boils,
    For my mental and bodily Pains,
For without them my Faith all congeals
    And I'm doomed to HELL'S NE'ER-ENDING FLAMES.

A SEVENTEENTH-CENTURY LOVE LYRIC

THE BLEWISH eyeballs of my love
  Are so enormous grown
The muscles, which the pupils move,
  Won't twist 'em round alone.

But lo! they hold an alien course:
  (I must myself outshine)
They yield to the magnetic force
  Of other stars than mine.

MOTHER AND I

The Child speaks:

"OH I have got a lovely book,
    'Tis brave and true and strong,
The date is on the title-page,
    I bought it for a song."

Mother: "And what is in your lovely book,
    My grave and gracious son?"
Child: "Oh, ev'rything that ever was
    Since this world was begun!"

Mother: "Now do not say you read all that,
    For if you read a lie
The gracious Lord will flutter down
    And peck away your eye.

And if you lie about your books
    He will remove your sight,
Or cover you with angry boils,
    And would He not be right?"

Child: "Oh yes, mamma! But here's the book
Upon the parlour table;
I could not lie about it, for
It is the HOLY BIBLE!"

FOR NINETEENTH-CENTURY BURIALS

THIS COLD weather
Carries so many old people away.
Quavering voices and blankets
    and breath
Go silent together.
The gentle fingers are touching to pray
Which crumple and straighten for Death.
These cold breezes
Carry the bells away on the air,
Stuttering tales of Gothic, and pass,

Catching new
grave flowers
into their
hair,
Beating the
chapel and
red–coloured
glass.

HE INDEPENDENT Calvinistic   1810
    Methodist Chapel is gone,
Dust in the galleries, dust on the stairs,
    There was no one to carry it on.
And a Norman New Jerusalem Church   1840
    Was raised on the sacred site,
Where they praised the Lord and praised
    the Lord
    By incandescent light.

The Gothic is bursting over the way
    With Evangelical Song,   1860
For the pinnacled Wesley Memorial Church
    Is over a hundred strong,
And what is a New Jerusalem
    Gas-lit and yellow-wall'd
To a semi-circular pitchpine sea
    With electric light install'd?

Crack your walls, Wesley Memorial!

Shine bright, you electrolier!

Your traceried windows may rock with song.

New Jerusalem fall in fear;

Short lived! Short lived! in this world of ours

Are Triumph and Praise and Prayer.

What of Mount Carmel Baptists (Strict), 1875

For they've central heating there?

THE SANDEMANIAN
MEETING-HOUSE IN HIGHBURY QUADRANT

ON ROARING iron down the Holloway Road
    The red trams and the brown trams pour,
And little each yellow-faced jolted load
    Knows of the fast-shut grained oak door.

From Canonbury, Dalston and Milmay Park
    The old North London shoots in a train
To the long black platform, gaslit and dark,
    Of Highbury Station once and again.

Steam or electric, little they care,
    Yellow brick terrace or terra-cotta hall,
White, wood, sweet shop or silent square,
    That the LORD OF THE SCRIPTURES is LORD OF ALL.

Away from the barks and the shouts and the greetings,
    Psalm-singing over and love-lunch done,
Listening to the Bible in their room for meetings,
    Old Sandemanians are hidden from the sun.

TUNBRIDGE WELLS

TUNBRIDGE WELLS on a Lord's Day
     Morning,
  Rung from rest by the Gospel Bells,
Climbs to light through the mist adorning
Towers and steeples of Tunbridge Wells.

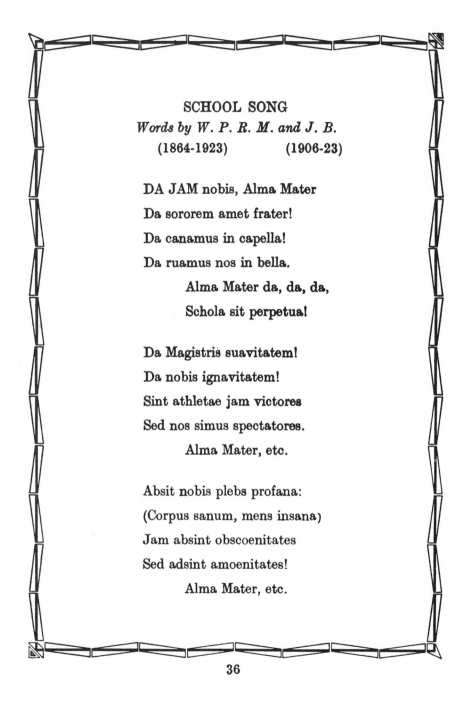

SCHOOL SONG

Words by W. P. R. M. and J. B.

(1864-1923)   (1906-23)

DA JAM nobis, Alma Mater

Da sororem amet frater!

Da canamus in capella!

Da ruamus nos in bella.

 Alma Mater da, da, da,

 Schola sit perpetua!

Da Magistris suavitatem!

Da nobis ignavitatem!

Sint athletae jam victores

Sed nos simus spectatores.

 Alma Mater, etc.

Absit nobis plebs profana:

(Corpus sanum, mens insana)

Jam absint obscoenitates

Sed adsint amoenitates!

 Alma Mater, etc.

36

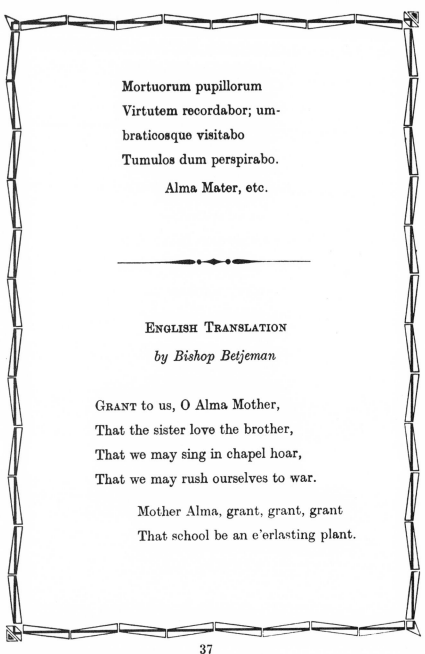

Mortuorum pupillorum
Virtutem recordabor; um-
braticosque visitabo
Tumulos dum perspirabo.

Alma Mater, etc.

ENGLISH TRANSLATION

by Bishop Betjeman

GRANT to us, O Alma Mother,
That the sister love the brother,
That we may sing in chapel hoar,
That we may rush ourselves to war.

Mother Alma, grant, grant, grant
That school be an e'erlasting plant.

37

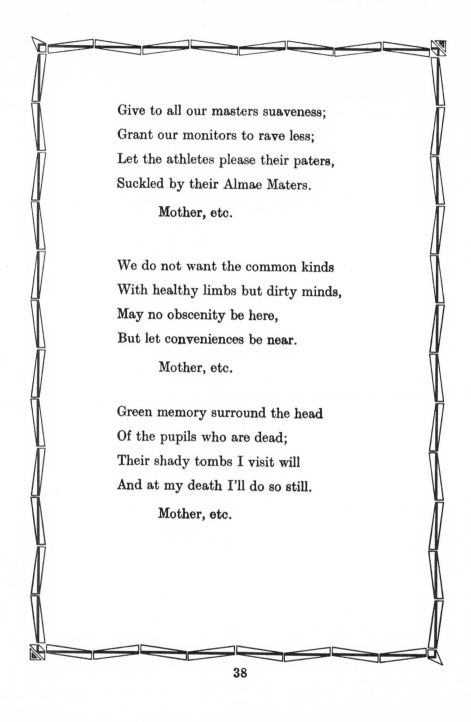

Give to all our masters suaveness;
Grant our monitors to rave less;
Let the athletes please their paters,
Suckled by their Almae Maters.

    Mother, etc.

We do not want the common kinds
With healthy limbs but dirty minds,
May no obscenity be here,
But let conveniences be near.

    Mother, etc.

Green memory surround the head
Of the pupils who are dead;
Their shady tombs I visit will
And at my death I'll do so still.

    Mother, etc.

CAMBERLEY

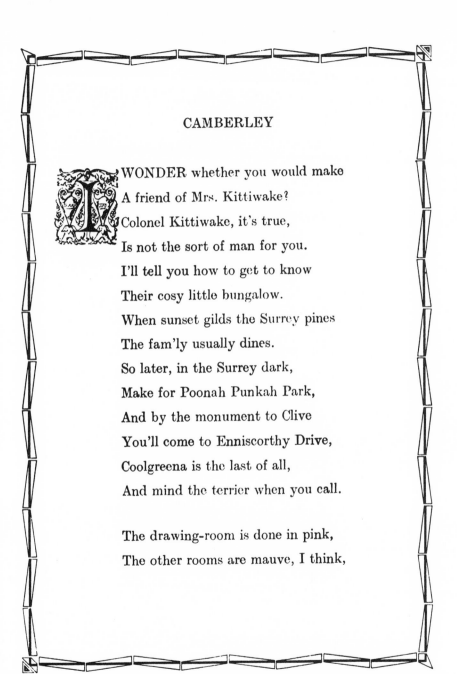

WONDER whether you would make
A friend of Mrs. Kittiwake?
Colonel Kittiwake, it's true,
Is not the sort of man for you.
I'll tell you how to get to know
Their cosy little bungalow.
When sunset gilds the Surrey pines
The fam'ly usually dines.
So later, in the Surrey dark,
Make for Poonah Punkah Park,
And by the monument to Clive
You'll come to Enniscorthy Drive,
Coolgreena is the last of all,
And mind the terrier when you call.

The drawing-room is done in pink,
The other rooms are mauve, I think,

So when you see electric light
Behind pink curtains it's all right.
Knock gently, don't disturb the maid,
She's got to clear, and I'm afraid
That she is less inclined to take
The blame than Mrs. Kittiwake.

ARTS AND CRAFTS

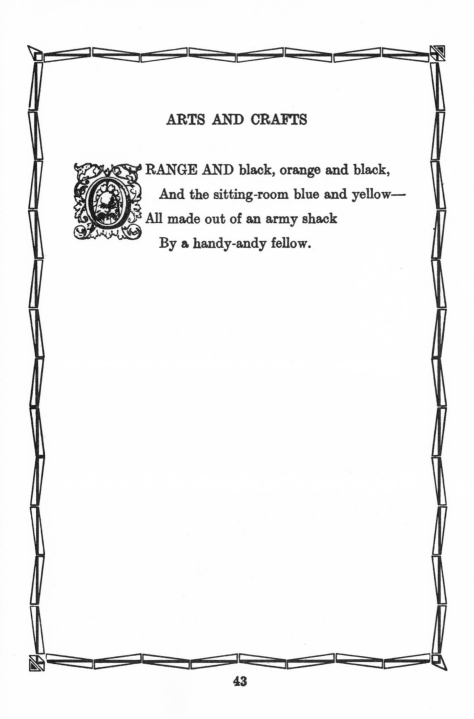

RANGE AND black, orange and black,
   And the sitting-room blue and yellow—
All made out of an army shack
   By a handy-andy fellow.

THE OUTER SUBURBS

THE WEARY walk from Oakleigh Park
Through the soft suburban dark
Bedizened with electric lights
Which stream across these Northern Heights.
In blackened blocks against the view
Stands gabled Rosslyn Avenue,
And bright within each kitchenette
The things for morning tea are set.
A stained-glass window, red and green,
Shines, hiding what should not be seen
While wifie knits through hubbie's gloom
Safe in the Drage-way drawing-room.
Oh how expectant for the bed
All 'Jacobethan' overhead!

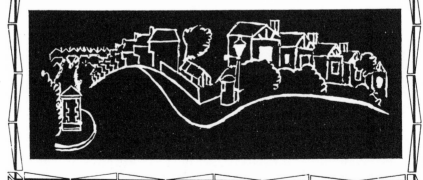

CROYDON

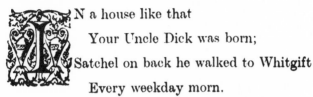N a house like that
Your Uncle Dick was born;
Satchel on back he walked to Whitgift
Every weekday morn.

Boys together in Coulsdon woodlands,
Bramble-berried and steep,
He and his pals would look for spadgers
Hidden deep.

The laurels are speckled in Marchmont Avenue
Just as they were before,
But the steps are dirty that still lead up to
Your Uncle Dick's front door.

Pear and apple in Croydon gardens
Bud and blossom and fall,
But your Uncle Dick has left his Croydon
Once for all.

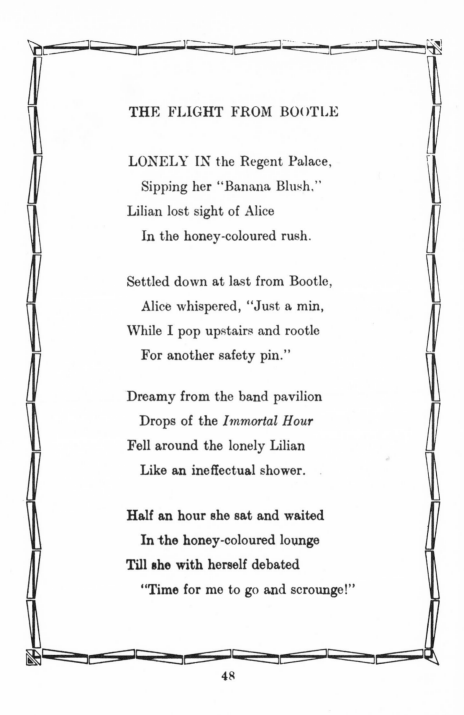

THE FLIGHT FROM BOOTLE

LONELY IN the Regent Palace,
Sipping her "Banana Blush,"
Lilian lost sight of Alice
In the honey-coloured rush.

Settled down at last from Bootle,
Alice whispered, "Just a min,
While I pop upstairs and rootle
For another safety pin."

Dreamy from the band pavilion
Drops of the *Immortal Hour*
Fell around the lonely Lilian
Like an ineffectual shower.

Half an hour she sat and waited
In the honey-coloured lounge
Till she with herself debated
"Time for me to go and scrounge!"

Time enough! or not enough time!
Lilian, you wait in vain;
Alice will not have a rough time,
Nor be quite the same again.

WESTGATE-ON-SEA

HARK, I hear the bells of Westgate,
    I will tell you what they sigh,
Where those minarets and steeples
    Prick the open Thanet sky.

Happy bells of eighteen-ninety,
    Bursting from your freestone tower!
Recalling laurel, shrubs and privet,
    Red geraniums in flower,

Feet that scamper on the asphalt,
    Through the Borough Council grass,
Till they hide inside the shelter
    Bright with ironwork and glass,

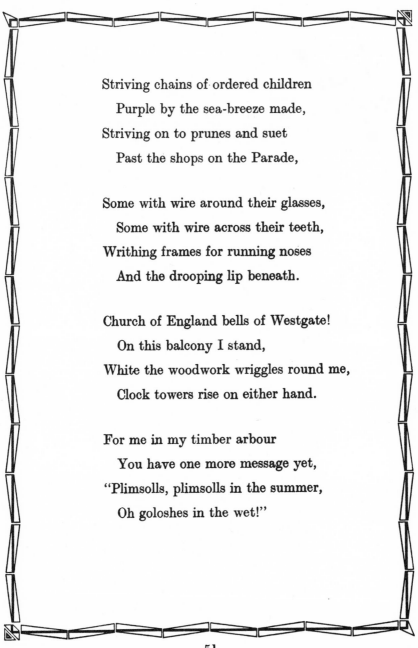

Striving chains of ordered children
　　Purple by the sea-breeze made,
Striving on to prunes and suet
　　Past the shops on the Parade,

Some with wire around their glasses,
　　Some with wire across their teeth,
Writhing frames for running noses
　　And the drooping lip beneath.

Church of England bells of Westgate!
　　On this balcony I stand,
White the woodwork wriggles round me,
　　Clock towers rise on either hand.

For me in my timber arbour
　　You have one more message yet,
"Plimsolls, plimsolls in the summer,
　　Oh goloshes in the wet!"

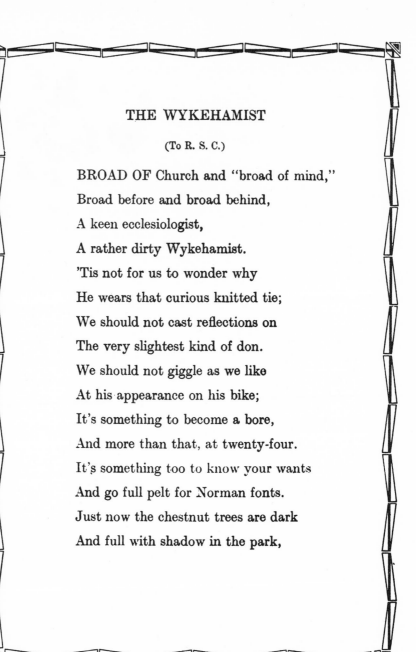

THE WYKEHAMIST

(To R. S. C.)

BROAD OF Church and "broad of mind,"
Broad before and broad behind,
A keen ecclesiologist,
A rather dirty Wykehamist.
'Tis not for us to wonder why
He wears that curious knitted tie;
We should not cast reflections on
The very slightest kind of don.
We should not giggle as we like
At his appearance on his bike;
It's something to become a bore,
And more than that, at twenty-four.
It's something too to know your wants
And go full pelt for Norman fonts.
Just now the chestnut trees are dark
And full with shadow in the park,

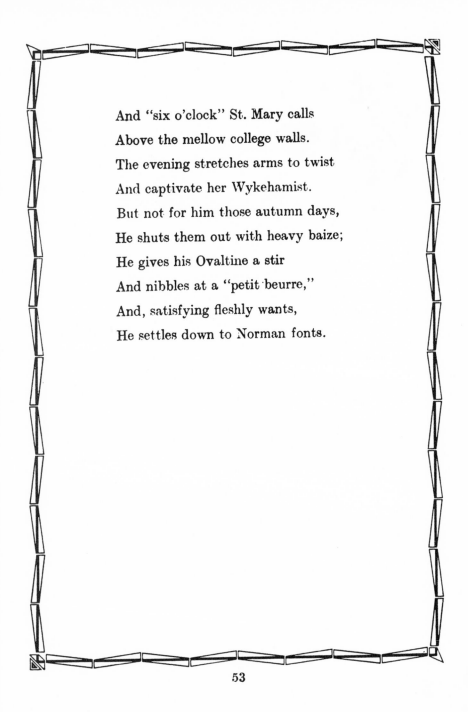

And "six o'clock" St. Mary calls
Above the mellow college walls.
The evening stretches arms to twist
And captivate her Wykehamist.
But not for him those autumn days,
He shuts them out with heavy baize;
He gives his Ovaltine a stir
And nibbles at a "petit beurre,"
And, satisfying fleshly wants,
He settles down to Norman fonts.

THE GARDEN CITY

WOT ye why in Orchard Way
   The roofs be steep and shelving?
Or wot ye what the dwellers say
   In close and garden delving?

"Belike unlike my hearths to yours,
   Yet seemly if unlike them.
Deep green and stalwart be my doors
   With bottle glass to fryke* them.

"Hand-woven be my wefts, hand-made
   My pottery for pottage,
And hoe and mattock, aye, and spade,
   Hang up about my cottage."

Men of Welwyn! Men of Worth!
   The Health Reform is growing,
With Parsley girdled round the earth
   That recks not of its sowing.

* Mediæval word for "deck."

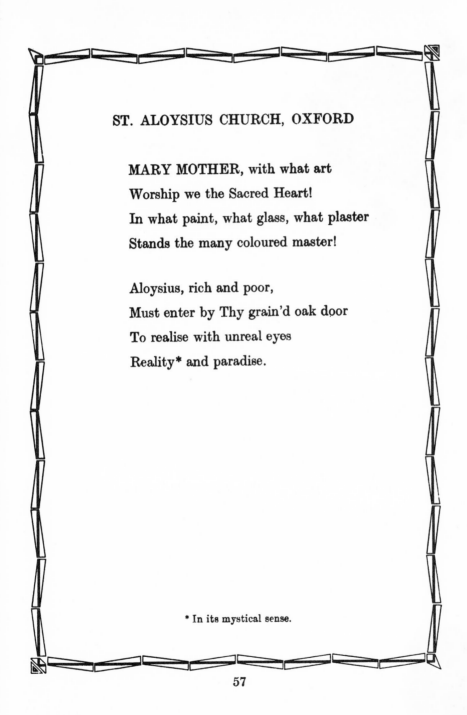

ST. ALOYSIUS CHURCH, OXFORD

MARY MOTHER, with what art
Worship we the Sacred Heart!
In what paint, what glass, what plaster
Stands the many coloured master!

Aloysius, rich and poor,
Must enter by Thy grain'd oak door
To realise with unreal eyes
Reality* and paradise.

* In its mystical sense.

The James Press
3 Culross Street
London